Contents

*Bonus Orchestral Listening Tracks: 30
- Beethoven's Symphony No. 6 in F Major
  Opus 68 (Pastoral): Gewitter, Sturm (Thunderstorm)   17
- Debussy's Clair de Lune (Moonlight) from
  Suite bergamasque   18

BEWARE THE MUSIC TEACHER!

Language Activity

Have the students listen to the recording and look at their lyric sheets to find these musical words in the song that have double meanings. See what musical definitions the children can decide upon, and then write the definitions on the board. Also discuss other (non-musical) definitions. If possible, show pictures of, locate, or demonstrate these words.

Instruments   devices used for producing musical sound

Sharp   to raise a pitch by a half step

Accidental   a flat, sharp, or natural placed in front of a note to show that it is different from the notes indicated by the key signature

Tuning fork   a metal device that, when struck, sounds a definite pitch

Horsehair   the type of hair on a bow that is drawn across string instruments, such as the violin, viola, cello, or string bass

Bow   a stick with horsehair attached that is used for playing string instruments such as the violin, viola, cello, or string bass

Frog   the part of the string player's bow that is held by the player

Horns   any of a variety of wind instruments, particularly the French horn

Scales   sequences of notes going up or down in pitch

Musical Activities

- Discuss how songs sometimes have an instrumental break or interlude when the singing stops but the instruments keep playing.
- Have children listen to the recording and raise their hands when they hear the instrumental interlude.
- Listen again and pat the steady beat during the instrumental interlude (eight measures).
- Discuss the tango* style, listening to the piano accompaniment on the recording.

- Have children move around the room during the interlude, walking to the steady beat.
- Have children walk four steps in one direction with arms pointing in that direction (tango-style) and then switch abruptly to the other direction for the next four beats. Continue doing the tango for the eight measures of the interlude.

* *The tango is a Latin-American ballroom dance in 2/4 or 4/4 time, or the music for this dance. Tango may also be a verb: let's tango! The tango was originally an African drum dance, possibly of Niger-Congo origin.*

BEWARE THE MUSIC TEACHER!

By
MARK BURROWS

Wait for introduction on CD.

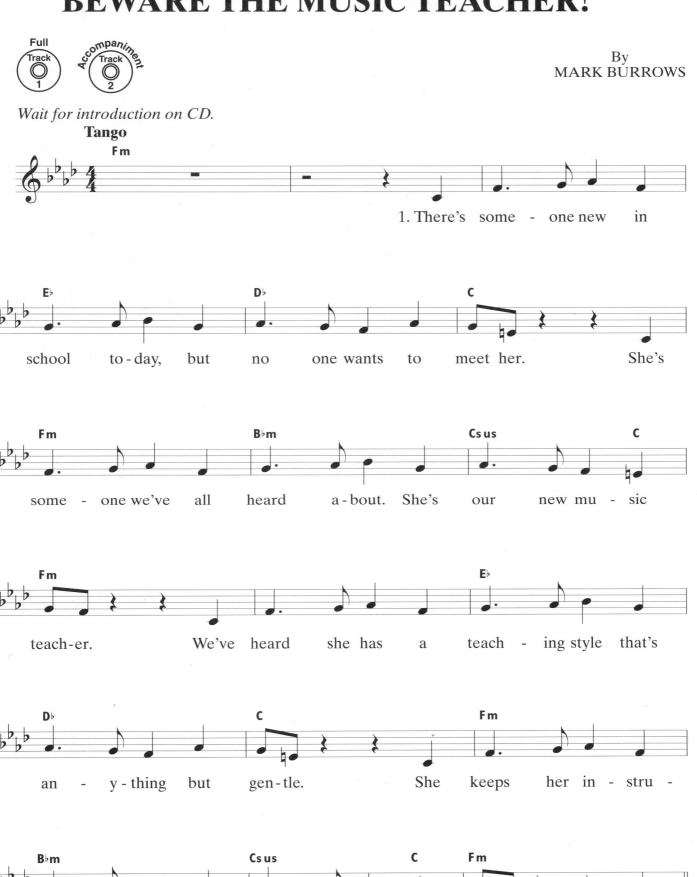

prod us with her tun - ing fork if we don't sing on
horn - rimmed glass - es are con - nect - ed by a string of

key. And then she'll make us beat the drums be -
pearls. Her bead - y eyes peer o - ver them to

fore she sets us free. We're way too old to
stare down boys and girls. We have - n't fig - ured

fear the dark, or an - y made - up crea - ture. But
out just yet her most spine - ting - ly fea - ture. But

one thing we can say for sure, "Be - ware the mu - sic
one thing we can say for sure, "Be - ware the mu - sic

2nd time To Coda

teach - er!"

Interlude:

2. We've

6

heard she is a sca - ry sight. The ru - mors just don't

stop. She wears her horse - hair in a bow and

puts a frog on top. We know that she's got

lots of horns, or so we've heard the tales. She's

al - so got an old pi - a - no co - vered all in

D.S. %al Coda Coda

scales. Her teach - er!" Yes, one thing we can

say for sure, "Be - ware the mu - sic teach - er!" *Yikes!*

7

BEWARE THE MUSIC TEACHER!

By Mark Burrows

There's someone new in school today, but no one wants to meet her.
She's someone we've all heard about. She's our new music teacher.

We've heard she has a teaching style that's anything but gentle.
She keeps her instruments quite sharp, but claims it's accidental.

She'll prod us with her tuning fork if we don't sing on key.
And then she'll make us beat the drums before she sets us free.

We're way too old to fear the dark, or any made-up creature.
But one thing we can say for sure, "Beware the music teacher!"

(Instrumental Interlude)

We've heard she is a scary sight. The rumors just don't stop.
She wears her horse-hair in a bow and puts a frog on top.

We know that she's got lots of horns, or so we've heard the tales.
She's also got an old piano covered all in scales.

Her horn-rimmed glasses are connected by a string of pearls.
Her beady eyes peer over them to stare down boys and girls.

We haven't figured out just yet her most spine-tingly feature.
But one thing we can say for sure, "Beware the music teacher!"

Yes, one thing we can say for sure, "Beware the music teacher!"
(spoken) Yikes!

The Boredom Blues

Music and Art Activity

The students can explore feelings in music. The blues is a style where music and words can come together to express feelings of sadness, loss, or even injustice.

- Using white construction paper and crayons or colored pencils, have the students respond to different musical moods. First, play an exciting, joyous piece of music such as the overture to Mozart's The Marriage of Figaro. Have students create a picture that illustrates the mood of the music.

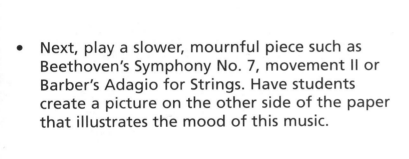

- Next, play a slower, mournful piece such as Beethoven's Symphony No. 7, movement II or Barber's Adagio for Strings. Have students create a picture on the other side of the paper that illustrates the mood of this music.

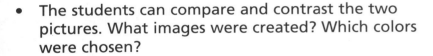

- The students can compare and contrast the two pictures. What images were created? Which colors were chosen?

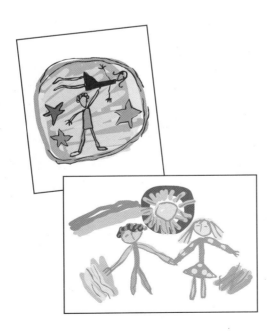

THE BOREDOM BLUES

By
MARK BURROWS

The Boredom Blues

By Mark Burrows

I've got the boredom blues, there's nothin' for me to do.

I've got the boredom blues, there's nothin' for me to do.

And if you sat around all summer, then you might be bored too.

I've spent six long weeks on summer vacation,

But still two weeks remain.

Then it's back to science and multiplication.

I can't wait for school to start again.

$3 \times 4 = 12$

$4 \times 4 = 16$

$5 \times 4 = 20$

$6 \times 4 = 24$

I've got the boredom blues, there's nothin' for me to do.

I've got the boredom blues, there's nothin' for me to do.

And if you sat around all summer, then you might be bored too.

In June I watched too much TV.

In July I twiddled my thumbs.

It's hard to think of anything good to do

When your mind has gone completely numb!

I've got the boredom blues,

    there's nothin' for me to do.

I've got the boredom blues,

    there's nothin' for me to do.

And if you sat around all summer,

    then you might be bored too.

Building a Bridge*

Musical Activity

Have students create a "river of sound."

- Give each student a piece of yarn, about 24 inches long.

- On a flat surface, have each student arrange his/her string like a river that flows from left to right. The river could wind up and down with lots of bends and curves, or be somewhat straight, with just a few contours. Each student's river will be different.

- Then have each student conduct his/her river of sound by tracing the path with his/her finger as the rest of the class vocalizes the river's every contour on "oo." The idea is to raise the singing pitch as the string (river) winds up and lower the pitch as the string goes down.

For variety

- Tie together pieces of yarn that are different colors so that one color starts where the other left off, and have the class make up new sounds for each color.

- Have the students decide which sounds correspond with each color of string. (This is like scoring for different colors of sound.) Not only will the students raise and lower pitch according to the direction of the string, but they will also change their tone color according to the color of the string; see examples below. Have fun and be creative!

- Choose a student to conduct the class's vocalise by tracing the string's path.

  Examples:
  - Blue - "oo"
  - Red - "ah"
  - Green - tongue clicks

- Have students devise many new sounds.

* The Lyric Sheet has been placed on page 13 to avoid page turns in the music.

Building a Bridge

By Mark Burrows

I look across the river and see you on the other side.
Then I wonder how the space between us ever got so wide.
I know we're far apart now, but I dream about the day,
When we can stand together. We've just got to find a way.

(Chorus)

Building a bridge between me and you is a job that is demanding.
It can't be built with rocks or steel, but with love and understanding.
And building a bridge between me and you will help us join each other.
And when we decide to cross it, we reach out to one another.

I smile across the river and I see you smiling too.
Now we see the task before us and we know just what to do.
We'll lay a firm foundation made of trust and honesty.
Then we'll reinforce with love to build a bridge of harmony.

(To Chorus)

We've built a bridge together,
and we've done our very best.
But now it's time to cross it.
We must put it to the test.

(To Chorus)

BUILDING A BRIDGE

By
MARK BURROWS

The Day the Animals Joined the Band*

Instrument-Making Activity

- Have students use their lyric sheets to locate all the instruments mentioned in the song:

harp horn  fiddle bongos stick rattle

- Have students bring items from home for use in making musical instruments such as rattles, bongos, or guiros. Rattles can be made using plastic bottles, jars, or cans filled with pebbles or plastic beads. Here's how you can make a guiro:

GUIRO

Materials needed:
- a cardboard tube (paper towel roll is a good size)
- ridged shelf liner
- 4 rubber bands
- an unsharpened pencil
- scissors

1. Cut shelf liner to the same length as the cardboard tube.
2. Wrap the shelf liner around the tube no more than two times.
3. Fasten the liner to the tube using rubber bands. (The longer the tube, the more rubber bands that will be needed.)
4. Scrape the ridges along the tube with the unsharpened pencil to make guiro sounds.

- Coffee cans, oatmeal containers, and/or plastic souvenir cups work well for bongos.
- Practice safety, making sure children do not put beads or pebbles in their mouths. Do not use cans with sharp or torn edges.
- Have students play their handmade instruments while singing "The Day the Animals Joined the Band."
- Dramatize the song, assigning an animal character to each student. Perform the song with the animals playing their instruments as they are mentioned in the song. On the last verse, ask the children to imagine they are a rock 'n' roll band!

Musical Extension

- Listen to the four-measure introduction on the CD. Discuss "walking bass."
  A walking bass line is a repeated bass pattern that seems to walk up and down a keyboard or bass instrument.
- Have students pat their laps to the steady beat of the walking bass.
- Have students pat up their sides as they hear the pitch go up, and down their sides as they hear the pitch go down.

* The Lyric Sheet has been placed on page 17 to avoid page turns in the music.

The Day the Animals Joined the Band

By Mark Burrows

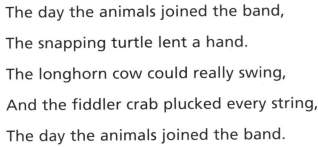

The day the animals joined the band,
The music rang throughout the land.
The harp seal strummed a lovely song,
While the humming bird hummed right along,
The day the animals joined the band.

The day the animals joined the band,
The snapping turtle lent a hand.
The longhorn cow could really swing,
And the fiddler crab plucked every string,
The day the animals joined the band.

The bongo and the walking stick,
They played a jumpin' beat.
The rattlesnake played with the rest
To make the band complete.

The day the animals joined the band,
There's never been a sound so grand.
They played all day. They played all night.
Oh, what a sound. Oh, what a sight!
The day the animals joined the band!

17

THE DAY THE ANIMALS JOINED THE BAND

By
MARK BURROWS

Wait for introduction on CD.

Rock 'n' roll with walking bass

1. The day the an - i - mals joined the band,___
(2.) day the an - i - mals joined the band,___
(3.) day the an - i - mals joined the band,___

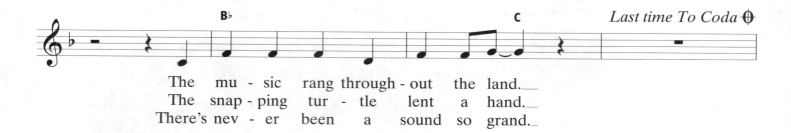

The mu - sic rang through - out the land.___
The snap - ping tur - tle lent a hand.___
There's nev - er been a sound so grand.___

The harp seal strummed a love - ly song,___ while the
The long - horn cow could real - ly swing,___ and the

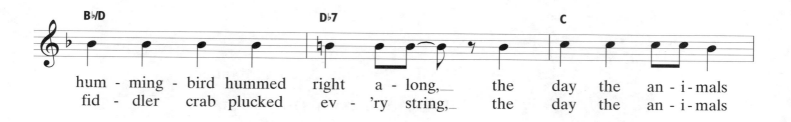

hum - ming - bird hummed right a - long,___ the day the an - i - mals
fid - dler crab plucked ev - 'ry string,___ the day the an - i - mals

joined the band.___
joined the band.___

2. The

18

The bon - go and the walk - ing stick, _ they

played a jump - in' beat. The rat - tle - snake played

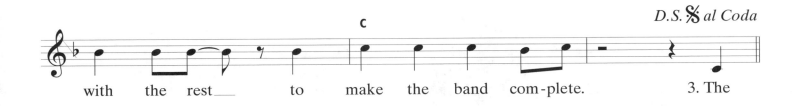

D.S. 𝄋 al Coda

with the rest _ to make the band com - plete. 3. The

⊕ *Coda*

They played all day. They played all night. _ Oh,

what a sound. Oh, what a sight! _ The day the an - i - mals

joined the band! _

Christmas Can Last All Year Long

Caring Activity

- Have the students create an audio holiday card.*
- Use a tape recorder to preserve the students singing of "Christmas Can Last All Year Long."
- Make several copies of the tape for people who would not otherwise be able to hear the students sing. You might want to send tapes to a local retirement center or children's hospital.
- Have students make and sign beautiful holiday cards to be sent along with the tapes.

*Please Note

1) Permission to make audio copies for this purpose has been granted by the Publisher and the Composer (Mark Burrows);
2) The copies may not be sold (only given away); and,
3) Under any other conditions, permission must always be obtained in advance from the copyright owners of any piece of music before copies of any kind are made and distributed (free or otherwise).

CHRISTMAS CAN LAST ALL YEAR LONG

By
MARK BURROWS

Wait for introduction on CD.

Christmas Can Last All Year Long

By Mark Burrows

When all the presents are opened,
When all the cards have been read,
When all the lights have been put away,
And the good will has been spread,

When all the white snow has melted,
When all the parties have passed,
When we return to our daily lives,
How can we make Christmas last?

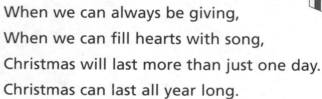

When we can always be giving,
When we can fill hearts with song,
Christmas will last more than just one day.
Christmas can last all year long.

When we can share with our neighbors,
When we can bring people cheer,
Then ev'ry day can be filled with hope,
No matter what time of year.

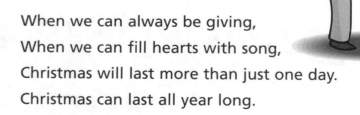

When we can always be giving,
When we can fill hearts with song,
Christmas will last more than just one day.
Christmas can last all year long.

Christmas will last more than just one day.
Christmas can last all year long.

Their Love Shines On

Musical Activity

The song "Their Love Shines On" uses the *e minor* scale. A scale can be identified by the pattern of pitches.

- Reproduce and hand out the lyric sheet for "Their Love Shines On," and ask students to look at the pitches for the *E Major* scale.

The pitches for the E Major scale are arranged like this:

E		F#		G#	A		B		C#		D#	E
	W		W	H		W		W		W		H

W = Whole Step
H = Half Step

The pitches for the e minor scale (natural minor) are arranged like this:

E		F#	G		A		B	C		D		E
	W		H		W		W	H		W		W

Notice that the pattern of whole steps and half steps is different for each scale.

- Have students look at the keys on a keyboard instrument as you play both scales several times.
- Ask students to describe the differences they hear.
- Have students close their eyes and guess whether you are playing the minor or the Major scale. Repeat this game several times.
- Next, simply play an *E Major* chord followed by an *e minor* chord.
- Once again ask students to describe what they hear; then play the guessing game with the chords.
- Have students listen to you play or sing the first few phrases of "Their Love Shines On" in *E Major* rather than *e minor*.
- Then ask students to sing the phrases with you.
- Ask students to describe how the mood of the song is changed. Which do they like better, *major or minor*? Take a vote!

Editor's Note: "Once Upon a December" from *Anastasia* is another lovely song about memories. It is also in a minor key. When we recall the past musically, do we usually do so in a minor key?

Additional Activity

- Have students make their own shoe box full of memories by collecting photographs of friends as well as some old pictures of family members. (You might want to plan this activity around the time students receive their school pictures.)
- Ask students to talk to their parents, grandparents, and other older family members to find out about their family history. They may want to look at photographs together to jog memories.
- Invite students to share their findings with the class.

THEIR LOVE SHINES ON

By
MARK BURROWS

Wait for introduction on CD.
Rolling ballad

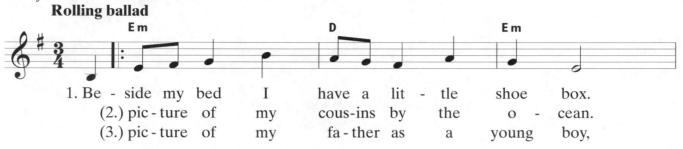

1. Be - side my bed I have a lit - tle shoe box.
(2.) pic - ture of my cous - ins by the o - cean.
(3.) pic - ture of my fa - ther as a young boy,

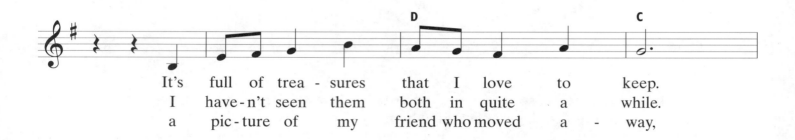

It's full of trea - sures that I love to keep.
I have - n't seen them both in quite a while.
a pic - ture of my friend who moved a - way,

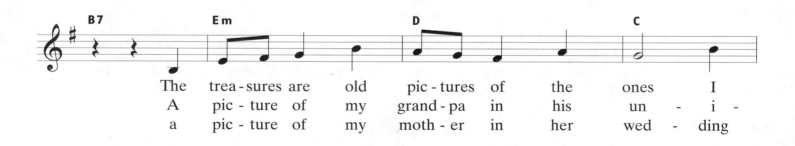

The trea - sures are old pic - tures of the ones I
A pic - ture of my grand - pa in his un - i -
a pic - ture of my moth - er in her wed - ding

love. I tell them all "Good - night" be - fore I
form. My grand - ma says that I have grand - pa's
dress. Some - how she gets more beau - ti - ful each

Chorus:

sleep.
smile.
day.

A shoe box full of mem - 'ries con -

nects me with the past, re - mind - ing me that some things will

al - ways last. Old im - ag - es of fam - 'ly, and

friends who've come and gone. Their pic - tures might have

fad - ed, but their love shines on. *rit. last time*

1.2.
2. A
3. A

3.

Their Love Shines On

By Mark Burrows

Beside my bed I have a little shoe box.
It's full of treasures that I love to keep.
The treasures are old pictures of the ones I love.
I tell them all "Goodnight" before I sleep.

Chorus:
A shoe box full of mem'ries connects me with the past,
Reminding me that some things will always last.
Old images of fam'ly, and friends who've come and gone.
Their pictures might have faded, but their love shines on.

A picture of my cousins by the ocean.
I haven't seen them both in quite a while.
A picture of my grandpa in his uniform.
My grandma says that I have grandpa's smile.

(To Chorus)

A picture of my father as a young boy,
A picture of my friend who moved away,
A picture of my mother in her wedding dress.
Somehow she gets more beautiful each day.

(To Chorus)

The pitches for the E Major scale are arranged like this:

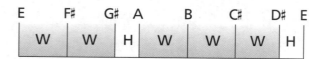

The pitches for the e minor scale (natural minor) are arranged like this:

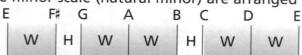

Notice that the pattern of whole steps and half steps is different for each scale.

Hola Means "Hello"

Musical Activity

The students can learn about communicating through music.

- Using body percussion, singing voices, or instruments, have each student create a musical way of saying "hello."
- As a call-and-response activity, have each student say "hello" musically (call), and then have the rest of the class echo "hello" in that same musical language (response).

Extension

- Create other musical phrases such as "See you later" or "Music is cool!"
- Lead a discussion on music as the universal language. Ask students why or why not they think music is the universal language.

HOLA MEANS "HELLO"

By
MARK BURROWS

Wait for introduction on CD.
Calypso/island beat

(Spanish) 1. Ho - la,___ ho - la.___ Ho - la means "Hel-lo."___
(Chinese) 2. Ni hao___
(Swahili) 3. Jam - bo___
(French) 4. Bon - jour___
(German) 5. Hal - lo___
(Hebrew) 6. Sha - lom*___

Ho - la,___ ho - la.___ Ho - la means "Hel-lo."___

Ho - la to___ my___ ma - ma.___ Ho - la to___ my___ pa - pa.___

Ho - la to___ my___ friends and___ ho - la to you.___

Ho - la,___ ho - la.___ Ho - la means "Hel-lo."___

Ho - la,___ ho - la.___ Ho - la means "Hel-lo."___

*"Shalom" also means "peace."

Hola Means "Hello"

By Mark Burrows

Hola, hola. Hola means "Hello."

Hola, hola. Hola means "Hello."

Hola to my mama.

Hola to my papa.

Hola to my friends and hola to you.

Hola, hola. Hola means "Hello."

Hola, hola. Hola means "Hello."

Repeat, singing "Hello" in these other languages:

Nǐhǎo (Chinese)

Jambo (Swahili)

Bonjour (French)

Hallo (German)

Shalom* (Hebrew)

*Shalom also means "peace."

Sing a Song for Nature*

Language/Social Studies Activity

- Have the students write a short story about their favorite animal and how it might deal with the threat of extinction. Students may use books, articles, or the Internet to get information.** (www.endangeredspecie.com is one Web site to explore.)
- Have students illustrate their stories or include a picture from a magazine, the Internet, or the newspaper, or the picture might be a real photograph. (www.webshots.com or www.zoonet.org are Web sites to explore.)
- As time allows, have some students read and show these to the class.

Music Listening Activity

Listen to recordings of classical music inspired by nature.

The following listening tracks are included on the CD with this book:***

Full Track 17   Full Track 18

- Beethoven's Symphony No. 6 in F Major, Opus 68 (Pastoral): Gewitter, Sturm (Thunderstorm)
- Debussy's Clair de Lune (Moonlight) from Suite bergamasque

Here are some other listening examples of music inspired by nature:

- Peter and the Wolf . . . . by Sergei Prokofiev
- The Creation . . . . by Franz Joseph Haydn
- The Seasons . . . . by Franz Joseph Haydn
- The Silver Swan . . . . by Orlando Gibbons
- The Cunning Little Vixen . . . . by Janos Janáček
- The Rite of Spring . . . . by Igor Stravinsky
- La Mer (The Sea) . . . . by Claude Debussy
- "Nuages" (Clouds) from Three Nocturnes . . . . by Claude Debussy
- The Blue Danube . . . . by Johann Strauss, Jr.
- Tales From the Vienna Woods . . . . by Johann Strauss, Jr.
- Alpine Symphony . . . . by Richard Strauss
- A Sea Symphony . . . . by Ralph Vaughan Williams
- Organ Concerto in F, No. 1, "The Cuckoo and the Nightingale" . . by George Frideric Handel

* The Lyric Sheet has been placed on page 31 to avoid page turns in the music. ☺

** For a script/musical presentation with CD and lots of information/pictures about endangered species, see Help the Animals! (BMR06016CD), published by Warner Bros. Publications, available from music or school supply stores.

*** More than 150 music listening tracks from all periods of music history are available with complete lesson plans in the Adventures in Music Listening series, published by Warner Bros. Publications, found at fine music stores.

Sing a Song for Nature

By Mark Burrows

LYRIC
SHEET
Full
Track
15

Accompaniment
Track
16

Who will speak the words for the flower?
Who will sing the song for the tree?
Who will blow the trumpet for the elephant
Hunted for his ivory?

Who will be the roar for the tiger?
Who will do the work of the bee?
For those who have no choice, we must be the voice.
We must help them to be free.
Yes, it's up to you and me.

Chorus:
Sing a song for nature.
Sing a song for all the earth.
Open your eyes and realize
How much our planet's worth.
Sing a song for nature.
Sing your whole life through.
If you sing a song for nature,
It will sing one back to you.

Who will be the shell for the turtle?
Who will save the chimpanzee?
Who will tell the tale of the great blue whale
Swimming in the great blue sea?
Yes, it's up to you and me.

(To Chorus)

Sing a song for nature.

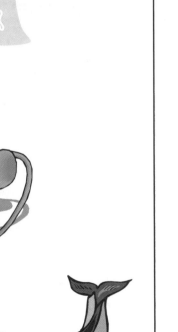
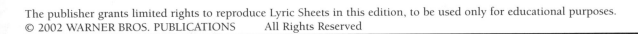

SING A SONG FOR NATURE

Unison (optional Two-Part)

Words and Music by
MARK BURROWS
Arranged by
RUTH ELAINE SCHRAM (ASCAP)

Wait for introduction on CD.

Sincerely

Who will speak the words for the flow - er?

Who will sing the song for the tree?

Who will blow the trum - pet for the el - e - phant hunt - ed

for his i - vo - ry?

Who will be the roar for the ti - ger?

Who will do the work of the bee? For

those who have no choice, we must be the voice. We must

sing one back to you.____

sing one back to you.____

(opt. Part I only)
Who will be the shell for the tur - tle?

(opt. Part II only)
Who will save the chim - pan - zee?

(All)
Who will tell the tale of the great blue whale swim-ming

poco rall.
in the great blue sea? Yes, it's up to you and

a tempo
me. Sing a song for na - ture.

Sing a song for all the earth. O - pen your eyes and

re - al - ize how much our plan - et's worth.

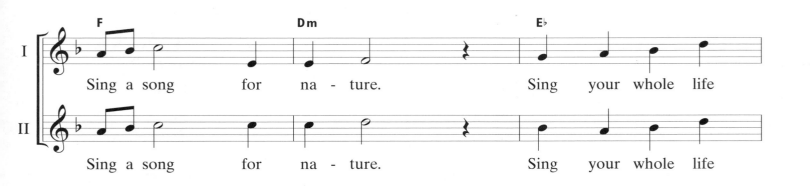

I Sing a song for na - ture. Sing your whole life

II Sing a song for na - ture. Sing your whole life

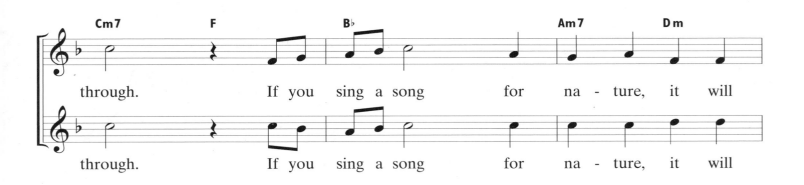

through. If you sing a song for na - ture, it will

through. If you sing a song for na - ture, it will

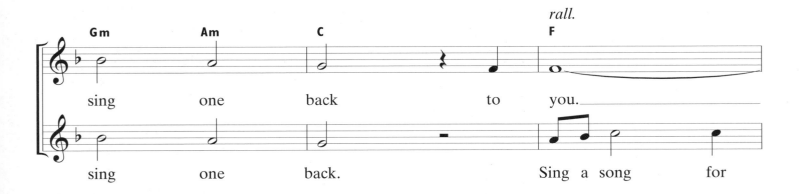

rall.

sing one back to you.

sing one back. Sing a song for

na - ture. Sing a song for na - ture.

na - ture. Sing a song for na - ture.

A Brand New Star in the Sky *

Musical Movement Activity

Use movement to express the lyrics in the song "A Brand New Star in the Sky."

Lyric	Movement
I'm the sunrise on the horizon.	Place one hand on top of the other, palms together. Then bring hands up together over the head. On "horizon," open hands out to either side in an arch.
I'm the bird that's learned to fly. 	Place one hand in a fist to represent a bird on top of the palm of the other hand; then lift both hands together and have the bird fly up high by waving that hand and arm.
I'm a bright new color in the rainbow.	Trace a rainbow arch over your head. (It's nice if everyone uses the same arm, such as the right.)
I'm a brand new star in the sky.	Starting with fists, on the word "star," flash open fingers of both hands in the air to depict sparkling stars.

Social Activity/Game

- Ask students if they have ever experienced difficulty putting their feelings into words.
- Select one student to come to the front of the room and secretly give that student an emotion to express, such as joy, anger, fear, calm.
- Instruct him/her to express that feeling through sounds only, without using any words.
- Have the other students guess which emotion is being expressed.

* The Lyric Sheet has been placed on page 37 to avoid page turns in the music.

A Brand New Star in the Sky

By Mark Burrows

I have a mind that's full of ideas.
I have a heart that's full of fun.
I have a smile as big as the world,
And a future as bright as the sun.

I'm the sunrise on the horizon.
I'm a bird that's learned to fly.
I'm a bright new color in the rainbow.
I'm a brand new star in the sky.

You are a very special person.
You have a light that's got to shine.
You are a true and wonderful friend
With a future as bright as mine.

You're the sunrise on the horizon.
You're a bird that's learned to fly.
You're a bright new color in the rainbow.
You're a brand new star in the sky.

We're the sunrise on the horizon.
We are birds that have learned to fly.
We are bright new colors in the rainbow.
We are brand new stars in the sky.

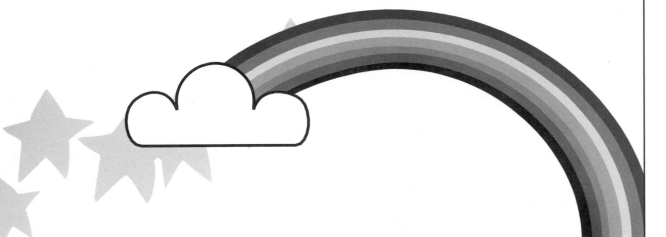

for Francine White

A BRAND NEW STAR IN THE SKY

By
MARK BURROWS
and the Fourth Grade Class at
Stephen C. Foster Elementary School, Dallas, TX

Wait for introduction on CD.

Up tempo

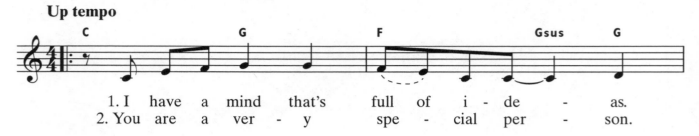

1. I have a mind that's full of i - de - as.
2. You are a ver - y spe - cial per - son.

I have a heart that's full of fun.___ I have a smile as
You have a light that's got to shine.___ You are a true and

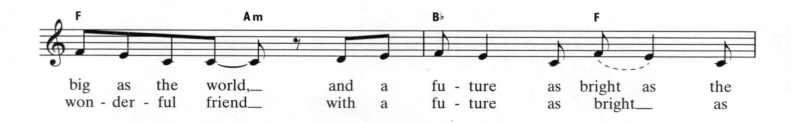

big as the world,___ and a fu - ture as bright as the
won - der - ful friend___ with a fu - ture as bright___ as

sun. I'm the sun - rise on the hor - i - zon. I'm a
mine. You're the sun - rise on the hor - i - zon. You're a

bird that's learned to fly. I'm a bright new col-or in the
bird that's learned to fly. You're a bright new col-or in the

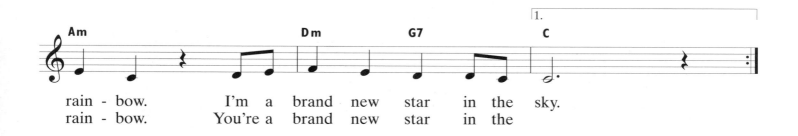

rain - bow. I'm a brand new star in the sky.
rain - bow. You're a brand new star in the

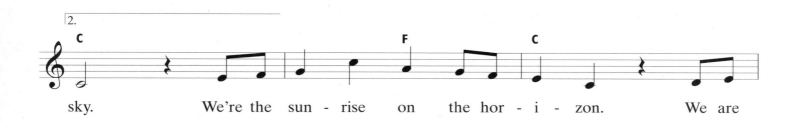

sky. We're the sun - rise on the hor - i - zon. We are

birds that have learned to fly. We are bright new col-ors in the

rain - bow. We are brand new stars in the sky.

(Positive) Attitude*

Creative Writing/Social Studies Activity

- Ask students to make a list of other **people who have made** a positive difference in the **world.**
- Then have students create new **verses to the song,** using the new list for inspiration. **Verses could also include members of the local community.**

Examples:

What helped Magellan guide his boat?
Attitude!

What helped Susan B. rock the vote?
Attitude!

What helped Elvis rock and roll?
Attitude!

What helped _____
(insert favorite football team) win the Super Bowl?
Attitude!

List people who have made a positive difference in the world:

1. _____

2. _____

3. _____

4. _____

5. _____

* The Lyric Sheet has been placed on page 41 to avoid page turns in the music. 🙂

(Positive) Attitude

By Mark Burrows

LYRIC SHEET
Full Track 21
Accompaniment Track 22

Attitude, positive attitude.
Attitude, positive attitude.

What helped Columbus cross the sea?
Attitude.
What helped Ford build the Model T?
Attitude.
What helped Beethoven write a tune?
Attitude.
What helped Armstrong walk on the moon?
Attitude.

When you know something that has to be done,
You've gotta go out and do it.
And when you have a positive attitude,
You'll find there's nothing to it.

What helped the Wright Brothers fly their plane?
Attitude.
What helped Gene Kelly sing in the rain?
Attitude.
What helped Doctor King have a dream?
Attitude.
What helped inspire ev'ry winning team?
Attitude.

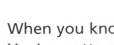

When you know something that has to be done,
You've gotta go out and do it.
And when you have a positive attitude,
You'll find there's nothing to it.

Attitude, positive attitude.
Attitude, positive attitude.

(POSITIVE) ATTITUDE

By
MARK BURROWS

Wait for introduction on CD.

got-ta go out__ and do it. And when you have a pos - i - tive

2nd time To Coda

at - ti - tude,__ you'll find there's noth-ing to__ it.

What helped the Wright Broth-ers fly their plane?__ At - ti - tude.__

__ What helped Gene Kel - ly sing in the rain?__

At - ti - tude.__ What helped Doc-tor King have a dream?__

At - ti - tude.__ What helped in - spire ev - 'ry

D.S. %. al Coda

win - ning team?__ At - ti - tude.__

Coda

At - ti - tude,__ pos-i-tive at - ti - tude.__

At - ti - tude,__ pos-i-tive at - ti - tude.__

We Are the Future, We Are the Now*

Music/Social Studies Activity

- Have students read and cut out newspaper and magazine articles (or locate them on the Internet) about young people making a positive impact in their communities. Make the classroom goal be to cover an entire bulletin board with the articles. The students can be inspired every day by seeing a collage of other children who are making a difference.

- **Discuss W. A. Mozart, a child prodigy:**
Wolfgang Amadeus Mozart was a great composer born in Austria in 1756. The son of Leopold Mozart, who was also a fine composer, young Wolfgang showed amazing talent at a very young age. He was already composing music at the age of five! By the age of six, he was touring Europe as a violinist and keyboard player. Mozart's life was filled with musical activity. He wrote more than 40 symphonies and several operas, including *The Magic Flute* and *The Marriage of Figaro*. Mozart died in 1791 at the young age of 35, ending a brief but brilliant musical career.

* The Lyric Sheet has been placed on page 45 to avoid page turns in the music. ☺

We Are the Future,
We Are the Now

By Mark Burrows

People always say, "The children are our future;
The leaders of tomorrow, not today."
But we can make a difference in the here and now
If you listen close to what we have to say.

Chorus:
We are the future.
We are the now.
We are the reason why.
We are the way how.
We have dreams to dream and lives to live.
We have love to share and help to give.
We can do whatever this world will allow.
We are the future.
We are the now.

Children of the world,
     we all must work together.
There's no time for us to hesitate.
Together we can make this world
     a brighter place.
We must start right now.
Tomorrow is too late.

(To Chorus)

We are people just like you,
With important things to do.
We don't want to sit and watch the time go by.
We feel sunshine; we feel rain.
We feel happiness and pain.
We can feel success if we're allowed to try.

(To Chorus)

WE ARE THE FUTURE,
WE ARE THE NOW

By
MARK BURROWS

About the Author

Mark Burrows

Mark Burrows received his undergraduate degree in music education from Southern Methodist University and his graduate degree in choral and orchestral conducting from Texas Christian University. Mark is currently the director of fine arts at First United Methodist Church in Fort Worth, Texas. He directs choral ensembles of all ages and oversees programs in visual arts and theater.

Prior to his work in Fort Worth, Mark was a music teacher at Stephen C. Foster Elementary School in Dallas, Texas. He has presented several local and national music workshops and is sought after as a conductor and clinician.

Mark resides in Fort Worth, Texas, with his wife Nina and daughters Emma and Grace.